Around
Countesthorpe
Revisited

Green Lane Cottages, *c.* 1910. The cottages were demolished in 1965.

BRITAIN IN OLD PHOTOGRAPHS

AROUND
COUNTESTHORPE
REVISITED

HENRIETTA SCHULTKA & ANN TRUE

The
History
Press

A view of Church Street looking west, showing the gates to the Baptist Chapel and The Manse, *c.* 1925. Both were built on manorial land.

First published 2011

The History Press
The Mill, Brimscombe Port
Stroud, Gloucestershire, GL5 2QG
www.thehistorypress.co.uk

ISBN 978 0 7524 5851 9

Typesetting and origination by The History Press
Printed in Great Britain

CONTENTS

ACKNOWLEDGEMENTS

Many of the photographs included in this book are part of Henrietta Schultka's personal collection. We would like to thank all those who generously donated additional photographs:

Norman Bazeley, Freda Dixon, John Orton, Margaret Blackwood, Muriel Harfield, Jennifer Harding, Margaret Hubbard, Eva Morris, Michael Root, Neta Wells, Sid Neale, the late George Dudley, the late Stanley de Peep, Jim Holden, Diana Winterton, Carol Chambers, Margret Thirlby, Beryl Beardsmore and the late Mildred Seares for their photographs of Countesthorpe.

The late Phyllis M. Stevens, the late George Worthey, the late Ken Vincent and the Garratt and Freer families for their photographs of Willoughby Waterleys.

Lorna Stevens, Peter Marshall, Bete Copson and Mrs Holes for their Peatling Magna photographs.

Maurice Copson, Margaret Godsmark and Kathleen Sheffield for their Peatling Parva photographs.

The Bruntingthorpe Heritage Group for photographs of their village.

Joan Gamble, Ella Hook and the late Elizabeth Kind for photographs of Kilby.

Diana Lee for photographs of Newton Harcourt. The Hon. Mrs Ann Brooks for her family photograph.

Also the Record Office at Wigston Magna.

INTRODUCTION

As many of us search for our family roots and discover photographs and documents that have been hidden in attics or cupboards, we uncover evidence that explains, intrigues and frequently surprises us. Unfortunately, some evidence is destroyed as we fail to realise the significance of what we have found.

With our heightened awareness of our personal history through television programmes such as *Who Do You Think You Are?*, a further question, 'Where do you think you come from?' becomes significant.

Revisiting Countesthorpe and its surrounding villages has allowed us to become more familiar with our heritage; to see how village life has developed, how villages have been relocated or even lost; how populations have grown or diminished and occupations altered to meet the demands of society.

Change is inevitable, yet looking back gives us the opportunity to evaluate our past and speculate on the future. Uncovering a range of new photographs of village life and lifestyles has allowed us to view the past in greater depth. The villages of Peatling Parva and Bruntingthorpe have been included in this edition to enhance our understanding of twentieth-century conventions and rural lifestyles.

Bruntingthorpe's original settlement was in the fields of Manor Farm, adjacent to St Mary's Church. It is thought that depopulation caused by the plague resulted in this site being abandoned.

Both Peatling Parva and Bruntingthorpe have their names recorded in the Domesday Book (1086). Peatling Parva was known as Alia Petlinge and Bruntingthorpe as Brandinestor. Agriculture played an important part in the lives of villagers in both communities and the changes in farming methods had an impact on each of the families. In 1870 there were eleven farmers working in Bruntingthorpe. In addition there were two grocers, two machine owners, a baker, butcher, builder, shopkeeper, grocer/draper, blacksmith, two tailors, a carriage builder, veterinary surgeon, wheelwright and carpenter, beer retailer, victualler/boot and shoe maker, and a victualler/carpenter. There were 423 souls recorded in the village.

In Peatling Parva in the same year there were eight farmers (three were non-resident), two boot and shoe makers, an innkeeper, grocer, shopkeeper, butcher, blacksmith, and a carpenter/wheelwright. There were 159 souls. These figures reflect a range of occupations in each village.

In the fifty years between 1870 and 1920, the population in six of the featured villages dropped considerably. Foston and Wistow remained approximately the same (forty and forty-nine respectively). Only Countesthorpe's population increased – from 1,000 to 1,473 – but this included officials, families and children in the City of Leicester's Cottage Homes.

Villages today are no longer self-sufficient: many are classed as dormitory, as people are more mobile and choose to live in different areas to where they work. As the pace of life intensifies and the pressures take on a different perspective, it is fascinating to look back at village life in a time gone by.

Ann True, 2011

 MARLBOROUGH HOUSE, S.W

12th June, 1951.

Dear Sir,

      Colonel Hedley Briggs has forwarded to me a package of nylon stockings of the kind which the Duchess of Kent saw when she visited your stand at the Leicester Industries Exhibition.

      I have today had an opportunity of showing these stockings to Her Royal Highness, who desires me to thank you for your kindness in sending them, and to say that she was very much interested to see them, and is glad to make an exception to her general rule by accepting them as a record of this visit. Her Royal Highness much appreciates your kind thought in sending this gift to her.

                  Yours truly,

                  Private Secretary.

P.M. Thompson, Esq.,
Messrs. Ashers (Hosiery)
           Ltd.,
Leicester.

A letter from the Duchess of Kent's Private Secretary following a visit to the Leicester Industries Exhibition. Thompsons (Ashers) Hosiery Ltd was based in Countesthorpe.

1

COUNTESTHORPE

The Fernie Hunt Meet in The Square at Countesthorpe in January 1935 at 11 o'clock. Factory owners would allow their workers to leave early to witness the event. They would probably have lunch before returning to work. The King William IV pub in the background was a George II farmhouse built in 1751 by John Gillam, a bachelor farmer.

Clearing of St Andrew's churchyard in The Square, *c.* 1951. The man seen in the photograph is Stanley de Peep from Cosby. Note the original brick wall around the churchyard.

This is the same view in 1955 when the changes to the churchyard can be seen. The buildings on the left were later demolished to make way for the Health Centre. The deeds for the farmhouse date back to 1690.

The interior of the King William IV pub before its refurbishment, *c*. 1985. The landlords at the time were Tony and Gina Pole.

The lounge bar where the Fearless Hiss & Boo band met to practise on Monday evenings. George Warner played the piano at lunchtime on Sundays.

Morris dancers performing in The Square in 1970.

Mrs Bailey is seen here pushing a pram with her son, Phillip, at her side. Gillam's farmhouse, centre right, is a well known feature of Countesthorpe.

This view shows the back of Gillam's farmhouse (the north side). It was called Gothic House on the 1851 census when the Humphreys family was in residence. It was owned by William Hope of Rushton Hall, Northamptonshire.

A rare photograph of St Andrew's Church in 1884, with the playground of the village school in the foreground. The box-framed house on the left stood where the Co-op car park is now.

Above: This interior shot of the church was taken around 1884 and shows what it was like before the alterations of 1907.

Left: The newly built chancel arch was constructed by the Chapman Brothers and was a feature of the 1907 alterations. Henry Chapman is on the left and Alfred George Tilley on the right.

This photograph from around 1930 shows the gas fittings in the chancel and reminds us how traditional the church looked with its wooden pews, brass lectern, organ, choir stalls and reading desks for the clergy. The pews were replaced by chairs in May 2004.

A new bell was made in 1925. There were originally four bells dated 1686, 1704, 1773 and 1816. These were re-cast and re-hung with the two new bells, making a ring of six bells.

In 1913 Henry Chapman & Sons (builders) constructed the extension of the Church School in Main Street. It was recently converted into housing.

Countesthorpe's old Co-op was demolished in May 1971; the new store can be seen on the right. The building on the left was the Co-op manager's house.

Main Street, *c*. 1890. Note the thatch on the central and right-hand buildings and the town pump on the left of what was then the butcher's. It later became Morris's and then Briggs Cycle Shop and General Store. The cottage on the far right has now had the rendering removed, showing the original timber framing of the box-framed house.

Bay Tree Cottage on Peatling Road was originally a blacksmith's shop on the road to Peatling Magna. Elizabeth Starkey gave it to her niece, Susanna Starkey, when she married John Ralphs, a blacksmith, of Dunton Bassett on 16 January 1697. It was then a four-and-a-half bay house with a cottage. Only one bay of this crook-framed house and two of the crooks have survived. Edwin George Hubbard and his son, Richard Edwin, are standing in the centre of this picture, taken around 1925.

The cobbled pavements of Wigston Street, c. 1932. The view looks north with the Axe and Square pub and the Methodist Church on the left.

This shot of Church Street shows local men with their wagons, c. 1925. They were possibly delivering bricks from one of the local brickyards.

Church Street (formerly Jacksons Lane), looking east. The houses on the left were demolished to make way for the car park next to the butcher's. The house in the centre was demolished to make way for Scotland Way and a bus stop. A detached house has replaced the house on the right.

This is the front view of the house in the previous photograph. It was the home of William Henry and Annie Ward in the 1950s. William (known as Henry) was a smallholder and carrier.

Taken around 1925, this photographis of Wigston Street looking towards The Bank. Note the wrought-iron gate on the left. The three houses between Glazebrook's factory and the corner shop were demolished to make way for the entrance to Dale Acre.

Henry Ward is standing behind the wall in Wigston Street. Note the village pump in the centre of the picture, one of a number in the village streets. The cottage on the left has been demolished. The wooden gate on the extreme left shows the entrance to Anderson's Yard.

Mrs Annie Ward (*née* Grant), wife of Henry, can be seen with their son, William Leeson, standing outside the Cromwell and Roseberry Villas on Wigston Street in the early 1900s. Annie was a schoolmistress at the Village School on Main Street.

This postcard of Foston Turnpike Road was post-dated December 1907. The detached house was named Thornleigh. During the Second World War, John Gordon Barrett, his wife Angela Mary and their family lived in the house. Their son, John Patrick, was a pilot sergeant in the 122 Squadron RAF (volunteer reserve). He died on 19 June 1942, aged 20.

This view is of the rear of Thornleigh in 1909, when it was the home of Walter James Sweet and his family. Walter and his wife ran the Axe and Square and the Bulls Head pubs at the same time during the First World War.

THE CEMETERY, COUNTESTHORPE

Countesthorpe cemetery looking north in the mid to late 1920s. Graves were allowed to settle for six months before the earth was built into a mound and turfed over, with a vase placed on it for flowers.

The photograph of Poplar's Farmhouse on Green Lane was taken around 1980. It was built on the site of a pre-enclosure farmhouse around 1890 by Mr John Thirlby, who later emigrated to Australia. John was a farmer born at Packington and was not related to builder George Thirlby.

This picture shows the north side of Poplar's Farmhouse (1982) before the demolition of two-thirds of the two-storey building to make way for the road into the new housing development (Poplars Farm Close).

Linden Farm, Station Road (previously Hall Lane), seen here in 1982. What appears to be a small Victorian farmhouse had, in 1767 at enclosure, 115 acres and 33 perches of land attached to it. The farm was owned by John Benskin, a non-resident landlord from Stony Stanton.

Farm buildings which were part of Linden Farm, 1982.

Cyril Ringrose, the owner, is standing to the right of the petrol pumps and workshop on Station Road. There is a workshop and second-hand car salesroom on this site today. This Ringrose family is a different one to Ringrose the Bakers, whose bakehouse was in Main Street.

This photograph shows the level crossing on Station Road, looking towards South Wigston, in 1962. The rail track had already gone due to Mr Beeching's cuts. The signal box and waiting room are in the background. Mrs Margaret Blackwood is standing on the platform.

Claude H. Smith and Jane Gayton were married at the Baptist Chapel on 24 April 1905. This photograph was taken outside the Gayton family home, a wooden bungalow, on Foston Road, Countesthorpe. The bungalow was demolished in the 1950s. The officiating minister was the Revd E. Yenn, and his son, Arthur, played the organ at the ceremony.

This wedding took place at St Andrew's Church on 14 June 1917. The groom is John Arthur Neale, a regular sailor, aged 29. The bride is Florence Annie Chapman, aged 22. Also pictured are Selena Rebecca Chapman, the bride's sister, and Edward Chapman, her father.

Children standing round a bomb crater behind the old council houses on Station Road on Good Friday 1941. The gardens of Nos 2 and 44 Bassett Avenue now occupy this site.

Members of the Countesthorpe Home Guard, *c.* 1942. The Home Guard was formed in 1940 and the men who volunteered were mostly those who were too old (over the age of 40) or too young (under the age of 18) to serve in the forces. Most of the men had full-time jobs and trained in the evenings. They were issued with a uniform and an armband with the letters LDV (Local Defence Volunteers) to show that they were members of the Home Guard.

This image shows the dedication of the banner of the Women's British Legion on 4 July 1938. Countesthorpe's vicar, Revd Canon H.V. Williams, is standing on the platform. Florence Tompkin Pollard (*née* Chapman) is holding the standard.

Taken at Bitteswell Park, Leicestershire, this photograph shows the D Camp 2nd Battalion Leicestershire Army Cadet Corps in 1942. From left to right: ? Reynolds (an evacuee); Gordon Burrell; George Munns; Robert Evans; Norman Gilliver.

The Neale brothers, seen here at Hunstanton, Norfolk, *c.* 1950. From left to right: -?-, Eddie, Sid, Alf. Eddie served in the RAF during the Second World War, while Sid and Alf did National Service. Sid went on to become a Chief Inspector in the Hampshire Police.

A group of surviving First World War soldiers at the Village Hall. Jack Herbert, seated second on the left, died in 1940.

A British Legion Parade on the way to St Andrew's Church, *c.* 1956.

Sheep shearing at Beeches Farm, Green Lane. Thomas Slawson Lowe is on the left and William Lowe is standing next to him with the dog. Note the mud wall in the photograph. Thomas Slawson Lowe died in December 1919.

This photograph shows Poplars Farm on Green Lane, *c.* 1926. Seated from left to right are Shirley Clarke; Mary Clarke; *?* Needham; Alfred Oldershaw; Reuben Page. The lady standing at the back is not known.

Seen here are two sons of the Clarke family of Poplars Farm. Shirley is on the left and Herbert on the right.

This picture shows the women knitters at Beale & Herberts Hosiery Factory & Dyeworks in Central Street, *c.* 1930.

The dyeing and finishing department at Beale & Herberts Hosiery Factory & Dyeworks can be seen here. The cottage industry of stocking knitting started in the village at the beginning of the eighteenth century.

The factory workers at Thompsons (Ashers) are shown celebrating with Wilford Lord on the occasion of his retirement. A letter was sent to P.M. Thompson on 12 June 1951 from the Duchess of Kent's private secretary. It mentioned her visit to their stand at the Leicester Industries Exhibition, where she was able to see their nylon stockings being made.

Seen here is Arthur Mould working as a labourer, possibly at Enderby, *c.* 1934. The lorry belonged to Henry Briggs of Countesthorpe.

Left: Staff at the Council School on Leicester Road pose for a photograph in the 1950s. From left to right, standing: Miss Davenport (teacher); Mr Gilliver (Headmaster); Mrs Bishop (dinner lady). Seated are Miss Jenkins (teacher) and Mrs Mildred Page (*née* Lee). Later on Miss Jenkins moved to Bogata to join her brother and to teach.

Below: A Countesthorpe Guides meeting at the back of Thornleigh on Foston Road, *c.* 1958. Among the group are Lieutenant Beryl Beardsmore and Captain Mildred Sears. Kneeling second from the left in the front row is Rosemary Connolly.

A group of Brownies in their traditional uniform, *c.* 1958. Diana Clark is on the far left. Mrs Sturgess is on the far right. Heather Pilgrim is wearing the white hat and shirt of a Sea Ranger.

A typical camp at Willoughby Waterleys. Ann Howsley is second on the left. Jenny Garratt is in front.

The Baptist ladies are seen here on an outing to Trentham Gardens, *c.* 1950. Three generations are represented in this photograph. They include members of the Austrin, Hickford, Hunt and Brown families.

This photograph shows an old scholars' reunion for the Ter-Jubilee celebrations in March 1955. Special services were conducted by the Revd W.S. Davies, who had been Minister of the church between 1931 and 1939.

The Women's Branch of the Conservative Association is shown here as winners of the Harborough Cup, 30 April 1935. From left to right: Dorothy Measures (*née* Lyons); -?-; Mrs Edith Skeffington; Mrs Hill (President, holding cup); Martha Immins (*née* Cox); Florence Pollard (*née* Chapman); Madge Thirlby (*née* Cook); Isabel Soars (*née* Harrold); Kathleen Martin (*née* Soars).

Mary Weston is seen here cutting the cake as she celebrates her 21st birthday at the Methodist School Room in 1936. She is the daughter of John Arthur (Jacky) and his wife Margaret Weston. Among those standing behind the table are Margaret Weston, a young Betty Shutch, Mary Weston, John Arthur, Louisa Elliott, Amy Kenney, Martha Ann Weston (*née* Gillam), William Weston.

The Operatic and Dramatic Society performed 'The Yeoman of the Guard' at the Village Institute, Countesthorpe between the 28th of February and the 3rd of March 1934.

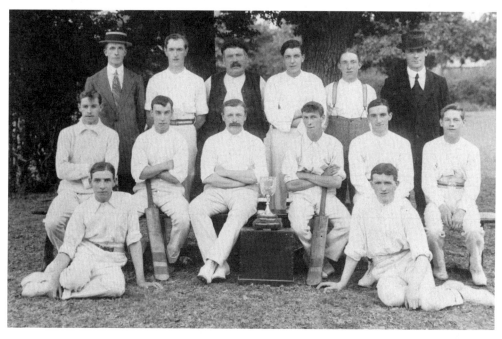

Countesthorpe cricket team, *c.* 1923. From left to right, standing: -?-; E. Boat; A. Warburton; E. Lord; P. Tompkin; Revd Williams. Middle row: W. Herbert; E. Warburton; T. Morris; S. Herbert; A. Tompkin; F. Herbert. Front row: Donald Peet; W. Tompkin.

The cricket team posing behind The Railway pub, either just before or just after the Second World War. Among those pictured in the back row are Mr Hickford, Ray Findley and George Wright (second from the right). Greg Findley is seated second from the left in the middle row. Aubrey Hickford is seated in the middle of the front row.

The Council School cricket first XI from Foston Road School, winners of the 1952 South Leicestershire Schools Cricket Cup. From left to right, back row: Michael Bell; John Ligo; Robert Lancaster; Richard Cosby; Neil Riddington (with shield); Melvyn Tattershall; Rodney Stretton; Malcolm Beerman. Front row: Roger Johnson; Malcolm Mould; Angela Stocker (scorer); Henry Hoskins. Mr Harold Gilliver (the Headmaster) is standing at the back.

Countesthorpe United Football Team, 1965. From left to right, standing: Arthur Cosby; John Atkins; Michael Barnett; Nigel Martin; Reg Bennett (goal keeper); Colin Root; John Clarke; Walter Elson (trainer). Kneeling: Robert Lancaster; Anthony Dudley; Ian Riddington; Roger Johnson; Alfred Stafford. Countesthorpe United played the Leicester City team, who played in the Cup Final at Wembley in 1949. The game was played on a field where Heather Way now stands.

Countesthorpe Ladies Hockey Team in the 1920s. Among those pictured here are Nellie Taylor; Jane (Jinny) Whitmore; Minnie Findley; Ethel Swan; Maggie Chapman; Maggie Taylor and Nellie Root.

Countesthorpe Bowls Club in the early 1960s. Dr Ethel Wynn Barnley (the village doctor) is seated on the left of the right-hand bench.

This photograph shows Leopold Wacks (a clothing manufacturer) with his wife Julia and their children. Leopold was born in Bristol and was living in Leicester by 1891. He was a prominent member of the Jewish Synagogue in Highfields. Julia was born in Stepney. They lived at Linden House from around 1920, for about five years. Leopold gave the land for the building of Countesthorpe Village Hall.

This picture, taken around 1976, shows Dr Trefor Goronwy, who was a part of the village medical team for several years.

Seen here is Thomas Meadows Gillam, the eldest son of Thomas Gillam and Elizabeth Robinson. He was born in Shearsby in 1804. This branch of the Gillam family lived in the large timbered house in The Square from 1604 to 1840. It was known as Gillam's Farm until 1915. Thomas Meadows emigrated to Western Australia around 1840 and married Elizabeth Jenkins.

Thomas's brother, William, the second son of this branch of the Gillam family, also emigrated to Australia.

Frank Raymond Thirlby can be seen here holding the Vitrix Ludorum award, *c.* 1936. He was a pupil at South Wigston Secondary School, Bassett Street.

Pupils from Linden Junior School, Gwendoline Drive, are photographed here during dress rehearsals for an historic pageant at De Montfort Hall, Leicester, in 1969.

Part of a fancy dress parade, *c.* 1953. The boys with the shields are Edward and Malcolm Duckett. Their mother, Mary, is standing behind and to the right of Malcolm.

This photograph shows the Golden Wedding party for Ivy (*née* Pettitt) and Ben (George) Berridge, who were the landlady and landlord of the Axe and Square pub for twenty-five years. They were married at Ellistown Parish Church in 1919. Mr Berridge was a miner for twenty-nine years prior to moving to Countesthorpe.

Seated in the centre of this photograph are Charles (a Midland Railway signalman born in Leicester) and Eliza Dorothy Higgs (from Ventnor, Isle of Wight), surrounded by their children, at the wedding of Edwin Felix Higgs (standing on the extreme right) in Spring 1906. His bride was Mary Elizabeth Hubbard.

Stalls at a Countesthorpe village fête, *c.* 1955. It was held in Henry Ward's fields where Brook Court/ Packman Green is now. As well as stalls, sports events and a fancy dress parade were organised.

2

WILLOUGHBY
WATERLEYS (WATERLESS)

This row of cottages on the road from Willoughby to Countesthorpe (looking south) was taken in 1982. They were originally farm labourers' cottages, owned by the Herbert family of Whetstone Pastures.

Right: Willoughby Waterleys Rectory, showing the conservatory built during the time of the Revd J.H.L. Jenkyns. Note the large stained-glass window, which is featured in a later photograph of 1920.

Below: An early photograph of St Mary's Church, *c.* 1900. This was taken before the porch around the north door was constructed in 1910, which was dedicated by the Bishop of Leicester.

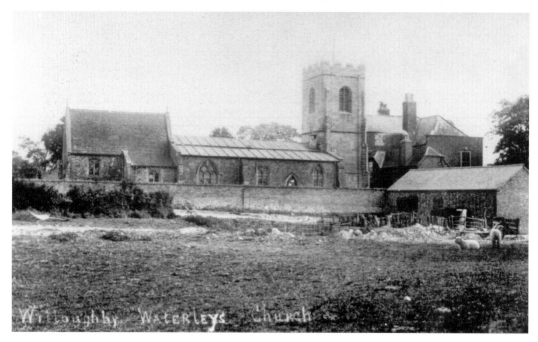

This picture shows the interior of St Mary's Church during a harvest festival, prior to the installation of electricity. According to the sales catalogue for the Rectory in 1944, 'an electric meter for Willoughby Church adjoining is placed on Rectory premises but separate meters could be installed ...'

John and Emma Mawby standing outside their house, which, at this time, had a roof of corrugated iron instead of its earlier thatch roof. Emma was buried on 16 March 1940, aged 81.

St. Mary's ✝ Parish Church
Willoughby | Waterleys.

The Rector and Churchwardens invite you on THURSDAY, MAY 12th (Octave of the F. of the Ascension), at 3 p.m., to

A Dedication Service
— BY —
The Lord Bishop of Leicester
— OF —

(a) NEW STONE PORCH.
(b) "INCARNATION" STAINED GLASS WINDOW (the generous gifts of Messrs Lowe and Family, of Countesthorpe).
(c) OAK ALTAR SANCTUARY RAILS (the generous gift of the Misses Herbert, of Leicester).
(d) ORGAN SCREEN (gift anonymous).

The Clergy are kindly requested to bring their Robes, and to meet in the Rectory Library, 2-30 p.m.

J. N. WORTHY, } Churchwardens.   J. L. H. JENKYN,
T. J. TURRELL, }   Rector.

SERVICES. 8 a.m. HOLY EUCHARIST.
3 p.m. DEDICATION SERVICE.
7 p.m. The Rev. JOHN GOODALL, M.A., R.D. Vicar of Rotherham (Canon of York Minster).

R.S.V.P. to Willoughby Rectory

An invitation to the dedication service of the additions to the fabric of the church in 1910; these were the new north stone porch, stained-glass windows, altar sanctuary rails and the organ screen.

St. Mary's ✝ Parish Church
Willoughby   Waterleys

In consequence of the Death of the King, the Bishop desires the

Postponement
—— OF ——

Dedication Services at St. Mary's
WILLOUGHBY,

To Thursday, May 26th.

SERVICES.

8 p.m. HOLY EUCHARIST.
3 p.m. DEDICATION SERVICE, with Address by THE LORD BISHOP OF LEICESTER.
7 p.m. EVENSONG. Preacher—THE REV. CANON GOODALL, M.A. (Vicar of Rotherham, and Canon of York Minster.)

The Rector and Churchwardens hope to see you present.
The Clergy are requested to meet at Rectory at 2-30 p.m.

R.S.V.P.

The dedication was postponed owing to the death of King Edward VII and rescheduled for 26 May, two weeks later.

This photograph shows the home of Rhoda Taylor and her daughter Caroline.

Rhoda was born in 1844, the youngest daughter of Joseph Taylor and Ann (*née* Warden), and died in 1926. Her daughter Caroline was born in 1862. Neither mother nor daughter married. Caroline died in 1947 and was the last member of the Taylor family to be buried in Willoughby Waterleys cemetery.

This aerial photograph of Willoughby looking north was taken around 1960. The road to the west by the Old Hall is to Ashby Magna; the road going east is to Peatling Magna; the road going north is to Countesthorpe.

A view of Main Street looking north and appearing very much as it does today.

Lockton's Yard, *c.* 1976. These cottages were constructed in 1630, partly of wattle and daub.

This picture shows Main Street around 1950. The Austin car (BJW 821) is displaying its AA badge, customary at the time. The image of the girls skipping along the road reflects a pastime of bygone Willoughby.

The motorbike (RC3671), seen outside the home of Jim and Lucy Vincent, belonged to their son, Ken Vincent. Jim was the last blacksmith in the village; their home was the house in the middle.

William Noel Worthey (always known as Noel) is pictured here with his invalid car, *c.* 1950. He was the son of George Herbert Worthey and Lily Maria. He was a cripple from birth and died at St Luke's Hospital, Market Harborough, on 24 November 1999, aged 78. He was buried at Willoughby Waterleys cemetery.

This photograph was taken around 1925. The building on the left of the picture later became the post office. Nene House is in the centre, to the right of the trees. The house and farm sold for £4,200 in 1944. The two-and-a-half-storey farmhouse on the right is now owned by the Attfield family and the land is farmed by them.

The Old Hall at the junction of the bridle road to Gilmorton and the road to Ashby Magna, *c.* 1925. In 1712 the house had been modified and enlarged by Richard Gamble. When it was auctioned in 1946, it was described as a 'charming old world residence' – electric light was installed, Leicester Water was connected; there was a hot water supply from an electric wash boiler (hired) and a telephone was installed. It sold for £1,550.

The north front of the Old Hall, *c.* 1920. The building was constructed on the edge of the village with a moat around it – all that remains is a pond.

The south front of the Old Hall, *c.* 1920.

A photograph showing the inside of the conservatory at the Rectory, *c.* 1920. Standing: Drucilla ? (housemaid); John Garratt (chauffeur/gardener); Mrs Sarah E. Ingham. Seated: Revd J.L.H. Jenkyns; Miss Jenkyns; Revd Ernest A. Ingham.

Seen here is Wilfred Hunt; the photograph is possibly taken at the time of his betrothal to Mary Archer, in 1911 or 1912. He worked as a gardener for the Herbert family at the large house at Whetstone Pastures. Mr Herbert owned an engineering factory at Coventry and was known as 'Millionaire Herbert'.

Mary Archer was a parlourmaid for Florence and Evelyn Herbert. They owned Pelham House on Welford Road, Leicester, but spent the summer at Gorse Farm, Whetstone Pastures. The sisters owned property in Willoughby and would have collected the rents in the summer.

This is Phyllis Hunt, daughter of Wilfred and Mary. She was born at Willoughby in 1914.

Seen here is Mrs Elizabeth Carr (*née* Warden) who was born at Willoughby in 1869. She lived in the cottage at the bottom of Church Lane. She married William Carr, the blacksmith, on 31 May 1887. Her father-in-law was William Marvin Carr.

Edwin Taylor, son of Silby Taylor and Ellen Elizabeth (*née* Cracknell). He was born in Willoughby on 2 November 1870. He was a fireman and later an engine driver on the Midland Railway. He died on 28 October 1958. The 1851 census shows that Elizabeth's father, David Cracknell, was the village schoolmaster at that time.

Edwin married Mary Isabella Taylor (pictured), the daughter of Martha Ilson and William Taylor, on 15 April 1895 at Willoughby Waterleys. Mary was baptised on 1 September 1861. She was buried at Wigston cemetery on 12 March 1918.

Private John Garratt of Thistle Hall (M/2/203343, Army Service Corps, 783rd Motor Transport Company). He was married to Ada Jane Tilley and was the chauffeur/gardener of Revd Jenkyns.

Private Edwin Warden (standing) and Ern (Ernest) Warden (seated). Edwin was in the 229th Employment Company. Because of his club foot, Ern was a shoemaker and not in the forces.

This photograph of Reginald Stevens was taken during the Second World War. Reginald was the son of Annie Stevens and was born at Countesthorpe around 1914. He later married Phyllis Hunt.

Kenneth Vincent during the Second World War. He was the son of James Vincent – a Methodist and the local blacksmith – and Lucy Gee. They were married on 24 December 1917.

Left: Nurse Claypole of Ashby Magna can be seen here outside the gate to the Old Hall, Willoughby, *c.* 1920. She was the District Nurse at Ashby Magna and Willoughby Waterleys.

Below: William Wesson cutting hay, *c.* 1922. He would take cattle to the Leicester Market on Wednesdays together with eggs and chickens.

Frances Elizabeth Wesson, sister of William. She may well have taken the duck eggs to the market, travelling with her brother.

These ladies are pictured at the Old Hall, Willoughby, c. 1920. From left to right, standing: Miss Baxter, Blanche Rogers, Miss Bennett, -?-. Seated: Miss Annie Baxter (Headmistress); Miss Florence Herbert of Whetstone Gorse; Edith Ellen Worthey (schoolmistress).

George Follows, a farmer, originally from Croft. He had farmed in several villages including Willoughby. He was born in 1865 and was buried on 25 February 1922. With him is his grandson, George Worthey, *c.* 1920.

John Norton Worthey, who lived at the Old Hall with his sister, Edith Ellen, was born in 1869. He was a churchwarden for many years. He died on 21 February 1922.

Willoughby Waterleys schoolchildren, *c.* 1895. Wilfred Hunt is on the far left in the back row.

The teacher seen here is Miss Annie Baxter, *c.* 1922. The girl in the striped dress, seventh from the left in the middle row, is Phyllis Hunt.

A wedding at the Methodist Church on 15 March 1969. The bridegroom is Peter Brian Groom and his bride is Penelope Ann Clements.

A fund-raising event (winter bazaar) held during the mid-1950s. The lady in the centre is Mary Hunt.

Harvest Festival at the Village Hall, *c.* 1959.

Willoughby Cricket Team in the 1930s. In the back row is the Revd Ingham. Second row, fourth from the right, with the cap on, is the scorer Ern Warden. Second from right, seated, with the cricket ball in his right hand is Wilf Hunt.

Left: Members of the Embroiderers Guild formed to create an embroidery depicting village folklore and fact. It was started in 1981 and includes field names, flora and fauna. Some houses of architectural interest appear in the letters of the village name.

Below: The exterior of the General Elliott public house. In 1846, Mary Ann Brown was a baker, shopkeeper and victualler of the General Elliott. In 1900 Henry Heath was the landlord; William Illson was a beer retailer.

The General Elliott pub sign. The pub was named after General Elliott (1717-1790), who was later Lord Heathfield of Sussex. He was victorious at the Siege of Gibraltar against the French and Spanish (1779-1783).

3

PEATLING MAGNA
(GREAT PEATLING)

An aerial view of the old village of Peatling Magna, looking north. Note the earthworks in the top right-hand corner.

This rare photograph shows the Bailey family at Great Peatling Lodge, *c*. 1900.

West Dale Farm (seen here in 1985), can be accessed via Austrey Lane, which is an old footpath/ bridleway to Peatling Magna from Countesthorpe. It can also be approached via Banbury Lane off the Willoughby Road.

This photograph of the cottages on the east side of Main Street was taken in the mid-1950s. Little has changed today.

This shows the junction of Main Street and School Lane.

Some of the last houses in Peatling Magna on the west side, looking north, taken in the mid-1950s. The Village Hall is in the centre of the houses.

A group outside the new Coronation Village Hall after the opening in 1911. Those standing include Charles Mawby, William Page, -?-, Frank Spokes, Elijah Jennings, Alfred Page, Miss Parr, George Parker, -?-, John Mawby snr, John Mawby jnr, Arthur Bacon and PC Cell. Seated from left to right are Dr Cowper (who lived in Blaby), Lady Dorothy Fraser, Mrs Cowper, and Sir Keith Fraser MP.

Standing behind the fence is Mrs D.E. (Bett) Copson, one of the village's last shopkeepers, talking to Mrs Eileen Wilson, *c.* 1963. The girl is Mrs Copson's daughter, Linda.

Main Street looking north, early 1950s. Note the name across the front of the building (The Cock Inn) – T.R. Buck & Sons, Lutterworth (brewery).

All Saints' Church, Peatling Magna, with Manor Farm on the left, *c.* 1895. The church is pictured here during restoration of the tower and spire.

This picture shows the interior of the church looking east from just below the tower, pre-1907. Note the font.

Above: The Jervis family were Lords of the Manor. The tombs shown here are unusual in that use has been made of alabaster. The inscription, from 1597, reads: 'Here lyeth the bodies of William Jervis and Katherine his wife which William deceased 8th Maye 1597 aged 94'. Sculptured on top and around the sides are their eighteen children, some of whom died in infancy (note the swaddling clothes).

Right: The inscription, from 1614, reads: 'Here lithe the bodies of William Jervis and Anne and Frances his wifes which Anne was daughter of Nicholas Purefoy of Drayton esquire which William had issue by her 2 sonnes and 3 daughters and deceased the 21 January 1614 aged 77'.

All Saints' Church in the 1950s. Manor Farm is on the right.

The interior of All Saints' Church in the 1950s, still with its oil lamps.

This picture shows the wedding of Maurice Copson and Doreen Elizabeth Kesterton on 1 October 1947.

The groom and his bride here are Norman Bazeley and Dorothy Kesterton, who married at All Saints' Church on 27 January 1951.

Raymond Dyson and Sylvia Kesterton celebrated their wedding on 2 March 1959. The Revd Peter Etchells officiated.

Guests of Mr and Mrs Dyson at their wedding reception.

Right: This is the Revd John Lloyd Hughs Jenkins BA, who was the vicar of Peatling Magna and the rector of Willoughby Waterleys. All Saints' Church was united with St Mary's at Willoughby in 1729. Jenkins was a precentor of Pro-Cathedral, Liverpool. He died on 19 July 1922 and is buried in Peatling Magna churchyard by the north door.

Below: Brookhill Farm with its portico still in place, in the early 1960s. The old houses are still standing today.

The Village, Peatling Magna

Main Street houses on the west side of the village in the mid-1950s. They were demolished around 1960.

Some of the last houses in Peatling Magna on the road going north out of the village, seen here in the 1950s.

Above: Lower Brook Hill Farm was owned by the Eales family, *c.* 1980. During the First World War the Chesterton family were tenant farmers here. Their youngest son, White Chesterton, died during the war and his name is on the war memorial. Thomas, the father, died in 1942. After his death, Trinity College Cambridge, the owners, sold the farm and land.

Right: Frank Edward Kesterton of the South Staffs Regiment, born in 1923. He was a prisoner of war in Japan for three years.

Above: Peatling Magna Home Guard in 1941. From left to right: Morris Tanser; Frank Spokes; Raymond Tanser (worked for Pollards); Noel Parker (worked for Pollards); Sgt Everett (cowman for M. Marshall).

Left: A Snapshot of Noel Parker, Percy Pollard, Albert and Sadie Hunt taken at Rose Cottage (next to the Cock Inn), *c.* 1950.

Above: Peatling Magna Women's Institute at Peatling House, *c.* 1945. Those standing include Mrs Hopkins; Miss A. Spokes; Mrs Haslan; Mrs Cheney; Mrs Perry; Mrs Flude; Miss P. Haslam; Miss F. Spokes; Miss K. Turrell (*née* Willoughby); Miss A. Marshall; Mrs Vesey; Miss P. Flude; Mrs R. Marshall. From left to right, sitting: Mrs Murray; Mrs Raven; Mrs Rippon; Mrs Busby; Mrs Kettell -?-; -?-; Mrs Boulter.

Right: Wedding of Harry Kesterton and Lillian Daisy Rest at Blaby Baptist Church 1911. They later moved to Peatling Magna in the late 1930s with nine of their surviving children. Harry died in 1940.

Samuel Tanser, his wife Margaret (*née* Mawby) and three of their children, Morris, Raymond and Ronald, in the mid-1930s. Samuel was the postmaster at Peatling Magna for forty years.

Percy Smith, a farm labourer for Attfields of Willoughby, reaping at Peatling Magna. He married Lillian Tanser.

4

PEATLING PARVA
(LITTLE PEATLING)

Peatling Parva Hall before extensive alterations, *c.* 1910.

The west side of Peatling Parva Hall, *c*. 1910. According to the 1851 census, it was occupied by James Buzzard, aged 37, his wife aged 34, their five children and forty-nine scholars. James was born at Smeeton Westerby and was a schoolmaster. Also living there were Edwin Potter, nephew and school assistant; Mary, his mother, aged 74; Henrietta, sister and housekeeper plus a cook maid, housemaid, and a kitchen maid.

St Andrew's Church and Attfield's Farmhouse, *c.* 1925. The latter was part of the Gemmel estate and was later demolished by the Gemmels.

This photograph of the interior of St Andrew's Church was taken by Mrs Moore of Clarendon Park, *c.* 1910. Note the oil lamps and the unusual triple chancel arches.

Harold Godsmark, aged 31, and Margaret Mary Jones, aged 20, were married at St Andrew's Church on 16 April 1949, which was Easter Saturday. The bride's veil was loaned by the then vicar's wife.

Opposite above: The home of Stephen Lee and his wife Fanny (*née* Measures) in the early twentieth century. She is standing in the doorway with their daughter, Agnes May. Stephen was the butcher for many years. Their eldest child, Thomas, was born in 1881 and was in the Leicestershire Yeomanry. His name is on the Peatling Parva War Memorial in the church, but no further information about him has been found.

Opposite below: The east side of the village looking north, pre-First World War. The village pub (The Shires) is in the centre of the photograph, but it is a much changed scene as a number of houses have been demolished.

This old thatched cottage was once the home of Aminda Maria Hubbard and her husband, John Thomas. It has since been demolished. Aminda was buried on 24 September 1942, aged 75 years. John was buried on 23 October 1946, aged 82 years.

The Village School and Old House, *c.* 1900. The 1901 census shows Miss M.E. Swanborough, a school mistress aged 46, living as a boarder in the village.

A later view of the school and cottages in Peatling Parva, looking towards the road to Ashby Magna from the Bruntingthorpe Road, in the early twentieth century. The photographer, Mrs Moore of Clarendon Park, was a prolific photographer of village scenes.

The school, Village Institute and cottages looking towards Ashby Magna from the Bruntingthorpe Road, c. 1914. The cows are being taken in for milking.

A later view of the previous photograph showing the school, Village Institute and cottages.

The Village Institute of Peatling Parva and District.

A farmhouse on the road from Peatling Parva to Bruntingthorpe, seen here in the early twentieth century. During the First World War, George and Ann Phillips farmed there. Their son died in the war. Note the two men in the front, one carrying a shotgun.

Mr Thomas William Copson, who was employed by Mrs Gemmel, is seen here driving the wagon on the Ashby Magna road with local girls in their May Day costumes, *c.* 1937. The May Queen was Pearl Richardson. Her attendants were Barbara Wilkinson and either Lorraine or Dora Sutherland. Two of the other girls are Margaret Godsmark and Pamela Hill. The boy is Donald Sutherland. Note the 'Autobell' ice-cream seller in the background.

5

BRUNTINGTHORPE

Main Street looking south, taken during the first decade of the twentieth century. 'Woodbine Cottage' and 'The Donkey Cart' are on the right-hand side. The house with the gable end onto the road, next door, was demolished to make way for The Plough car park. The licensed victualler of The Plough in 1900 was William Hickley. The last brick house on the right, called The Meet, was where members of the Hunt met to enjoy a stirrup cup. It was previously called Top End. The houses on the left, where the girls are standing, have since been demolished.

On the left of this early 1930s pictures is one of the few shops in Bruntingthorpe at the time, a general store selling items from sweets and groceries to kettles. The white house facing the photographer has been demolished. Home Farm is on the right.

Rose Cottage, Church Walk, *c.* 1900. Constructed in the period between 1550 and 1600, the original building was possibly a farm. It was a three-bay box-framed construction with a thatched roof. The shutters offered protection from the weather and possibly passing cattle.

Left: William Hobill (1836-1913) was a bricklayer's labourer and framework knitter. He married Hannah Broadwell in 1858. According to family lore, they lived in Rose Cottage for most of their married life and had eight children. The youngest, Priscilla (Kilworth) was buried in the churchyard in 1935. The 1901 census shows William Hobill (aged 63) living next door to the pub (The Joiner's Arms) with his son-in-law, Walter Kilworth, (a blacksmith), his daughter Priscilla and his granddaughter, Cicely, aged 2.

Below: The Joiner's Arms (also known as The Carpenter's Arms), *c.* 1900. In the trade directory of 1863, Benjamin Herbert is recorded as a joiner and victualler of The Joiner's Arms. In 1900 George Tarratt was the licencee. He is recorded as being the publican in the census of April 1901 (aged 37) but he died soon after and was buried on 7 August 1901. He had lived on the premises with his wife Harriett, aged 34, and his sons Charles, aged 5, and George, aged 3.

A later view of The Joiner's Arms with Mr and Mrs Baker standing outside, *c.* 1910. According to the late Jack Binder, a resident of Bruntingthorpe from 1941 to 1977, when the RAF moved into the aerodrome during the Second World War, The Joiners was used mainly by the flying crew and officers and the men used The Plough.

The Rectory, which was rebuilt in 1771-1776 on the site of a supposed sixteenth-century moated house. This was burned down in 1771 after a fire in the brewhouse. Frederick Bridges (rector from 1869-1881) added a new wing to the rectory. He is shown as living there with his family in both the 1871 and 1881 census.

Above: Bruntingthorpe Church – St Mary's – was rebuilt with the exception of the lower parts of the tower, which were underpinned. The work was completed in 1873 and has been virtually unaltered since. Centenary celebrations of this rebuilding were reported in the local newspaper on 25 March 1973. It is interesting to note that either Thomas Freeman or his son, George John Freeman, both rectors of the parish, seem to have altered the dedication of the church from St Mary to St Nicholas sometime between 1811 and 1846. In the 1875 trade directory, the church is referred to as St Mary once again.

Left: Albert Ernest Saunders and Doris Kilworth, who were married at St Mary's Church on 5 December 1931.

Beresford House, seen here on the right-hand side of Main Street, was auctioned on 2 December 1959. It was described as 'a commodious dwelling house', constructed of brick with a slate roof. It had an oak-beamed kitchen and an inglenook fireplace. On the opposite side of the street, the Barn is visible (by the car) and below it, White House Farm, Rose Cottage and School Farm.

This photograph shows White House Farm with its barn attachment – a late seventeenth-century timber-framed building with brick infill to all the panels. The house of three bays is now stuccoed. The barn of seven bays (dated 1714) at the rear, was rebuilt in the 1970s.

This picture shows the crowning of Carol Porter as the May Queen in the School Rooms in May 1950. Celebrating May Day was a colourful occasion in the village calendar and the children enjoyed parading through the village streets.

Children standing outside the village school. A National School was opened in 1871 for sixty children, supported by voluntary contributions. In 1900 the average attendance was forty pupils. The schoolmistress was Miss Edith Bird. She appears in the 1901 census, aged 34, as a boarder in the village. It is interesting to note that the school was closed at 3 p.m. on 20 September 1940 for the reception of twenty-five evacuees and their teacher, Mrs Fox. There were then three classes in the school.

A group of schoolchildren with teacher Miss Bullock from Smeeton Westerby on the left and Head Teacher Mrs Walden from Willoughby Road, Countesthorpe, on the right. Apparently both teachers travelled to school on mopeds and later Mrs Walden had a car. According to local residents, she and her husband also ran a youth club in the village.

Seen here is a group of WI ladies dressed up for their parts in a play, 23 May 1958. Those identified are Betty Mason (*née* Hearn), Sibil Baker, Una Green, Winnie Burke (*née* Kilworth) and Joyce Day.

Bruntingthorpe Cricket Team. From left to right, standing: -?- (umpire), Horace Bryan, Hubert Higgs, Horace Hickley, Fred Wild, Albert Jones, Eddie Jennings. Front row: Billy York, Reg Kilworth, Ernest Hickley, Jack Heard, Frank Cooper.

Main Street looking south as you leave the village. The Old Post Office is on the left with White Cottage next door. The Old Post Office was originally two cottages built in 1884. In 1941, it had no running water, only the pump in the garden, but it did have electricity. Water was installed at the end of 1941. The toilet was about 20 yards from the back door. The cottages on the right (known locally as Navies Cottages) have since been demolished. Beresford House can be seen beyond the trees.

6

FOSTON AND KILBY

These cartoons of the Hunt at Foston, drawn by Charlie Hammond in 1899, were found in his sketchbook in Australia and sent to the owners of Foston Hall Farm. They read: 'Cunnard hounds passing through Hall Farm on their way to Peatling Cover to draw. Chaff cutting had to wait – or join the glad throng.'
'I am told that I am going galloping mad and following in the footsteps of my father.' A GREAT RIDE FROM FOSTON TO ARNESBY.

St Bartholomew's Church, the rectory next door, Hall Farm, a row of cottages and a few isolated houses are all that remain of the village of Foston. Inside the church, against the north wall, is this large monument which commemorates Henry Faunt (son of Anthony Faunt) and his wife Elizabeth. Henry died in 1665 aged 84. It was Anthony Faunt who began to enclose the common land, causing villagers to leave and the village itself to eventually become deserted. The church is still active and Henry Faunt's monument is seen here decorated for the annual flower festival.

The farmhouse of Orlando Vann Hunt on Main Street, Kilby, *c.* 1890. According to the 1851 census, Orlando farmed 290 acres.

A photograph of Orlando Vann Hunt, who was born in 1813 in Thurnby, the son of John and Sarah Hunt. He died on 3 January 1880 in Leicester, leaving a personal estate of just under £3,000 in his will.

Mrs Elizabeth Hunt (*née* Sarson) was born in 1809 at Stoughton, the daughter of Edward Sarson. She married Orlando on 9 November 1843. After her death, Orlando married Sarah Wykes, a widow, on 7 January 1876.

Elizabeth Ann Hunt, daughter of Orlando and Elizabeth, who married James Goodman Elliott, aged 43, on 23 December 1873. Elizabeth was born around 1844 in Kilby and was baptised at Kilby Church.

Farmer James Goodman Elliott, son of Thomas Elliott and Mary Payne. He was born around 1830.

Above: A snapshot of St Mary Magdalene Church, Kilby, *c.* 1900.

Right: The wedding of Graham Gibson and Florence Nora Bowers at Kilby Church on 26 June 1936. At the time of writing, Florence is still alive and celebrated her 100th birthday in March 2010.

Members of St Mary's Church in the early 1920s.

Brook Bridge, Kilby, *c.* 1906.

Main Street, looking east, *c.* 1905.

Cottages on the south side of the village on the road leading out to Countesthorpe.

The house used as a post office in Kilby. It was the home of the Aldgate family in the 1920s. It was demolished to make way for the entrance to the Dog and Gun car park.

A view of Main Street from the junction with Wistow Road, *c.* 1930. The post office and the general store are on the right.

Above: Pupils and teachers at the village school, *c.* 1910. The school was erected in 1875 for fifty-seven children; the average attendance was forty-eight.

Right: Mr Jonathan Glover, *c.* 1880. A farmer at Kilby, he was born in 1834 and lived at Kilby Lodge. He farmed 725 acres and employed twelve men and four boys. His wife, Elizabeth, came from Market Harborough.

Alison, Olive and Ruth Chapman of Kilby in the early 1930s.

The Fernie Hunt Meet at Kilby, *c*. 1914. Many of the men who joined the hunt would have gone to war.

7

NEWTON HARCOURT
AND WISTOW

Lock-keeper's cottage and boat on the Grand Union Canal, *c.* 1955. The canal was fully opened in 1814 when coal was available at Kilby Bridge. At that time it cost between 9 1/2*d* and 11*d* per cwt.

The lock-keeper's cottage near Newton Harcourt in 1962. The Leicestershire & Northampton Union and the Grand Union Canals were sold to the Grand Junction in 1894. Joseph Falkner was the lock keeper in 1912.

Tythorn House in Newton Harcourt. This farmhouse burned down around 1950.

Above: An early postcard of Hurst's Farmhouse.

Right: The post office, with Edwin Freestone and his wife Annie Elizabeth in the doorway. Edwin was born at Newton Harcourt and Elizabeth was born at Arnesby. Edwin was a cordwainer (shoemaker) like his father Thomas, and by 1891 he was also the postmaster.

The Manor House, home of the Goddard family, pre-1910.

The wedding of Herbert Lonman, aged 30, and Annie Maria Bent, aged 31, at Newton Harcourt Church on 4 March 1919.

A traditional 1950s wedding – this photograph shows the bride, Mary Groom, and the bridegroom, John Smith, on their wedding day in either 1957 or 1958.

Farm labourer Bernard Bent outside his house. He owned the first car in Newton Harcourt.

This photograph shows Mrs Gertrude Wyatt, John Garner, Joyce Bent and Gwen Wyatt gathering in the coal, *c.* 1930. It was always delivered at the side of the road.

John Wyatt, Gertrude's husband, a farm worker.

It is believed this tractor was owned by the Wistow estate, which had land in the adjoining villages of Newton Harcourt, Fleckney and Kilby. The tractor was being produced between 1910 and 1920 and was the first in the world, predating the American version. The firm of 'IVEL' in Bedfordshire was started in the 1890s and combined with Saundersons in 1920.

Maypole dancers in the early 1930s.

Above: Villagers in fancy dress in the 1950s.

Opposite: Eliza Louisa Asher, seated, with a friend believed to be Miss Barsby; both were born at Kilby. This photograph was taken in the back of the post office garden at Newton Harcourt. Soon after, Eliza emigrated to Australia, where she tragically died.

Eliza Louisa Asher, aged 56, was one of forty casualties who died on 3 November 1927 following the collision of the ferry steamer *Greycliffe* with the Union Steamship Company's liner *Tahiti. Greycliffe* was bound for Watson's Bay and *Tahiti* was outward bound for San Francisco. After the collision, the ferry steamer was cut in two and sank immediately. This picture of Eliza's grave was sent to Nancy Scotchbrook (*née* Asher), her eldest sister.

The south front of Wistow Hall, *c.* 1904.

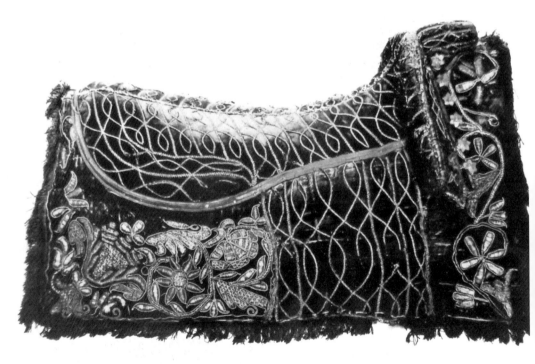

The crimson velvet saddle of Charles I which was left at Wistow (together with that of Prince Rupert) when King Charles slept at the Hall on 4 June 1645, ten days before the fateful battle of Naseby. The king's horse guards were quartered at Kilby and Foston. The saddles were probably left as a present, as Wistow was the home of Sir Richard Halford, an ardent Royalist. Charles I was executed on 30 January 1649.

Major Henry St John Halford of Wistow Hall, seen here in the late 1850s/early '60s. He was the commanding officer of the county's Rifle Volunteers between 1862-8 and 1878-91. He was Companion of the Bath for both local and national service and for thirty years his name was synonymous with the volunteer movement in Leicestershire. On his 60th birthday, the officers of the battalion gave him a maxim gun which he in turn presented to the battalion.

Sir Timothy Brooks KCVO, and the Hon. Lady Ann Brooks, pictured after Sir Timothy's retirement as Lord Lieutenant of Leicestershire from 1989 to 2003. Wistow Hall was passed on to Ann by her father, the 4th Lord Cottesloe, in 1958 and over the years, she and her husband restored and modernised the house. It has now been converted into a number of apartments but is still their family home. Timothy Brooks was High Sheriff in 1980, a post held by a previous owner of Wistow Hall, Richard Halford, some 370 years earlier, during the reign of James I.

A postcard of St Wistan's Church, Wistow, sent to Miss Emma Louisa Asher from her neice Louisa Scotchbrook of Newton Harcourt, 30 November 1905.

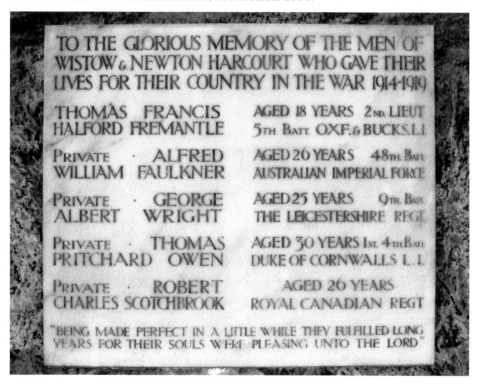

TO THE GLORIOUS MEMORY OF THE MEN OF WISTOW & NEWTON HARCOURT WHO GAVE THEIR LIVES FOR THEIR COUNTRY IN THE WAR 1914-1919

THOMAS FRANCIS HALFORD FREMANTLE	AGED 18 YEARS 2ND LIEUT 5TH BATT. OXF.& BUCKS.L.I
PRIVATE · ALFRED WILLIAM FAULKNER	AGED 26 YEARS 48TH BATT AUSTRALIAN IMPERIAL FORCE
PRIVATE · GEORGE ALBERT WRIGHT	AGED 25 YEARS 9TH BATT THE LEICESTERSHIRE REGT
PRIVATE · THOMAS PRITCHARD OWEN	AGED 30 YEARS 1ST 4TH BATT DUKE OF CORNWALLS L.I.
PRIVATE · ROBERT CHARLES SCOTCHBROOK	AGED 26 YEARS ROYAL CANADIAN REGT

"BEING MADE PERFECT IN A LITTLE WHILE THEY FULFILLED LONG YEARS FOR THEIR SOULS WERE PLEASING UNTO THE LORD"

The War Memorial for the men of Wistow and Newton Harcourt who were killed or who died of their wounds in the First World War. This can be found in the church. In addition there are three men, whose names are missing, who were all born at Newton Harcourt: J.A. Robins who was a stoker 1st class in the navy, who died on 30 December 1919 and is buried in Newton Harcourt churchyard. Frederick Arthur Jennings of the 1st and 4th Leicesters who died on 17 October 1918, aged 23 years. Thomas Harrold Sutton of the Royal Army Service Corps who died of his wounds in August 1921, aged 38 years.

Seen here on their wedding day, 20 June 1942, are Harry Arthur Hammond and Margaret Edith Tyrrell.

This view of the steam train with the canal in the foreground was taken in 1962. It had obviously been a hard winter as the ice-breaker had been used on the canal.

Other titles published by The History Press

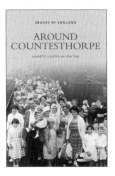

Around Countesthorpe
HENRIETTA SCHULTKA & ANN TRUE

This fascinating collection of over 200 old photographs depicts people, scenes and events from everyday life in the villages of Countesthorpe, Willoughby Waterleys, Peatling Magna, Foston, Kilby, Newton Harcourt and Wistow. Countesthorpe was an open village with no principal landowner. Non-conformity had a particular influence on its residents and the images of the village reflect this diversity. Local personalities and customs are featured, together with scenes of agricultural life, developing modes of transport, the unique Cottage Homes and elements of both world wars.

978 0 7524 1556 7

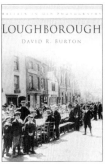

Loughborough
DAVID BURTON

Loughborough in Old Photographs records the growth from a small market town to a popular destination for students, housing one of the country's leading universities for sports education. David R. Burton has drawn together unique images from the archives of the Loughborough Monitor and Leicester Mercury. This book is an important record of the development of Loughborough and offers a wonderful insight into the past for residents and visitors alike.

978 0 7524 4978 4

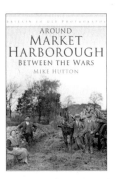

Around Market Harborough between the Wars
MIKE HUTTON

The inter-war years are a world away from what we are familiar with today; it was a time when it was possible to identify people by their dress, and youngsters were brought up to know their place. Working people had to endure long hours for poor pay in crowded factories. Farm labourers toiled for lower wages still, without any form of security. Mike Hutton's new book evokes these days beautifully, through many previously unseen photographs and his informative text. *Around Market Harborough Between the Wars* is sure to be of great interest to all those who know and love this historic Leicestershire town.

978 0 7524 4965 4

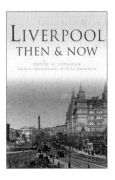

Liverpool Then & Now
DANIEL K. LONGMAN

The popular tourist city of Liverpool has a rich heritage, which is uniquely reflected in this fascinating new compilation. Contrasting a selection of forty-five archive images alongside full-colour modern photographs, this book delves into the changing faces and buildings of Liverpool. As well as delighting the many tourists who visit the city, *Liverpool Then & Now* will provide present occupants with a glimpse of how the city used to be, in addition to awakening nostalgic memories for those who used to live or work here.

978 0 7524 5740 6

Visit our website and discover thousands of other History Press books.

www.thehistorypress.co.uk